♡ Filthy Coupon Request ♡

Let me tie your hands behind your back. Get on your knees & lick my pussy (don't forget to lick my arse hole)

Present this coupon to your other half (during an argument is probably not the best time). Vouchers can be used more than once in instances where both parties have thoroughly enjoyed the filthy activities that the said coupon has suggested. These coupons are for the sole pleasure of a consenting couple. They are fully flexible and can be interpreted by each couple as they please.

(01) 0 9501101 53000 3 (17) 140704 (10) AB 123

♡ *Filthy Coupon Request* ♡

Today I am your servant and will let
you dominate me. Spanking, Slapping..
whatever you fancy!

(01) 0 9501101 53000 3 (17) 140704 (10) AB 123

♥ Filthy Coupon Request ♥

foreplay: suck on my breasts and play with them for 15 minutes.

(01) 0 9501101 53000 3 (17) 140704 (10) AB 123

❤ *Filthy Coupon Request* ❤

ROLE-PLAY: I AM A VIRGIN, AND THIS IS MY FIRST TIME.

Present this coupon to your other half (during an argument is probably not the best time). Vouchers can be used more than once in instances where both parties have thoroughly enjoyed the filthy activities that the said coupon has suggested. These coupons are for the sole pleasure of a consenting couple. They are fully flexible and can be interpreted by each couple as they please.

(01) 0 9501101 53000 3 (17) 140704 (10) AB 123

♡ Filthy Coupon Request ♡

Role-play: Pretend you're a teacher, I am the student who's trying to seduce you (so you can raise my grade.)

Present this coupon to your other half (during an argument is probably not the best time). Vouchers can be used more than once in instances where both parties have thoroughly enjoyed the filthy activities that the said coupon has suggested. These coupons are for the sole pleasure of a consenting couple. They are fully flexible and can be interpreted by each couple as they please.

(01) 0 9501101 53000 3 (17) 140704 (10) AB 123

♡ Filthy Coupon Request ♡

Suck on my pussy while I suck on your balls.

(01) 0 9501101 53000 3 (17) 140704 (10) AB 123

♡ *Filthy Coupon Request* ♡

Get the coconut oil out, its about to
get real filthy. Lay me on my tummy
& oil up my arse hole. Then we can
go from there...

(01) 0 9501101 53000 3 (17) 140704 (10) AB 123

♡ Filthy Coupon Request ♡

Let's watch some lesbian porn
together. Go down on me. It
turns me on watching you get
excited about me watching other
women.

(01) 0 9501101 53000 3 (17) 140704 (10) AB 123

♡ Filthy Coupon Request ♡

Role-play: I am a stripper. Give me money while I dance for you.

Present this coupon to your other half (during an argument is probably not the best time). Vouchers can be used more than once in instances where both parties have thoroughly enjoyed the filthy activities that the said coupon has suggested. These coupons are for the sole pleasure of a consenting couple. They are fully flexible and can be interpreted by each couple as they please.

(01) 0 9501101 53000 3 (17) 140704 (10) AB 123

❤ 𝓕𝓲𝓵𝓽𝓱𝔂 𝓒𝓸𝓾𝓹𝓸𝓷 𝓡𝓮𝓺𝓾𝓮𝓼𝓽 ❤

Let's watch porn naked while I am on all fours, you behind me. Let's see how long we last.

(01) 0 9501101 53000 3 (17) 140704 (10) AB 123

♡ Filthy Coupon Request ♡

You will be a male stripper this evening; You will dance for me. No touching (for the first 10 minutes)

(01) 0 9501101 53000 3 (17) 140704 (10) AB 123

♡ Filthy Coupon Request ♡

I will dress up as my favorite Disney princess, and you can fuck me really rough.

(01) 0 9501101 53000 3 (17) 140704 (10) AB 123

♡ Filthy Coupon Request ♡

Cover my body in oil, then give me a massage, using your hands and then balls.

(01) 0 9501101 53000 3 (17) 140704 (10) AB 123

♡ Filthy Coupon Request ♡

Role-Play: Pretend you are my servant. Kiss my feet & wait for my instructions.

(01) 0 9501101 53000 3 (17) 140704 (10) AB 123

♡ Filthy Coupon Request ♡

You go down on me, lick around my arsehole, then slowly suck on my clit. Keep one finger in my arse.

Present this coupon to your other half (during an argument is probably not the best time). Vouchers can be used more than once in instances where both parties have thoroughly enjoyed the filthy activities that the said coupon has suggested. These coupons are for the sole pleasure of a consenting couple. They are fully flexible and can be interpreted by each couple as they please.

(01) 0 9501101 53000 3 (17) 140704 (10) AB 123

♥ Filthy Coupon Request ♥

Let me dominate you. I will use my belt/rope/tie to tie your hands.

Present this coupon to your other half (during an argument is probably not the best time). Vouchers can be used more than once in instances where both parties have thoroughly enjoyed the filthy activities that the said coupon has suggested. These coupons are for the sole pleasure of a consenting couple. They are fully flexible and can be interpreted by each couple as they please.

(01) 0 9501101 53000 3 (17) 140704 (10) AB 123

Filthy Coupon Request

Foreplay: Let me lay across your lap and spank me for 10 minutes.

(01) 0 9501101 53000 3 (17) 140704 (10) AB 123

♡ Filthy Coupon Request ♡

Rim Job for you.

(01) 0 9501101 53000 3 (17) 140704 (10) AB 123

♥ Filthy Coupon Request ♥

Role-play: You are the Doctor. I am the patient.

Present this coupon to your other half (during an argument is probably not the best time). Vouchers can be used more than once in instances where both parties have thoroughly enjoyed the filthy activities that the said coupon has suggested. These coupons are for the sole pleasure of a consenting couple. They are fully flexible and can be interpreted by each couple as they please.

(01) 0 9501101 53000 3 (17) 140704 (10) AB 123

♡ Filthy Coupon Request ♡

Let me watch you masturbate while
I sit in front of you, legs open
with only my heels on.

(01) 0 9501101 53000 3 (17) 140704 (10) AB 123

♡ Filthy Coupon Request ♡

Foreplay: Intense kissing ONLY for 15 minutes.

Present this coupon to your other half (during an argument is probably not the best time). Vouchers can be used more than once in instances where both parties have thoroughly enjoyed the filthy activities that the said coupon has suggested. These coupons are for the sole pleasure of a consenting couple. They are fully flexible and can be interpreted by each couple as they please.

(01) 0 9501101 53000 3 (17) 140704 (10) AB 123

♥ Filthy Coupon Request ♥

Film me while I suck your dick.
(We can delete it after)

(01) 0 9501101 53000 3 (17) 140704 (10) AB 123

♡ Filthy Coupon Request ♡

Go down on me while I watch porn on my phone. I will describe whats going on while you are busy playing with my pussy.

Present this coupon to your other half (during an argument is probably not the best time). Vouchers can be used more than once in instances where both parties have thoroughly enjoyed the filthy activities that the said coupon has suggested. These coupons are for the sole pleasure of a consenting couple. They are fully flexible and can be interpreted by each couple as they please.

(01) 0 9501101 53000 3 (17) 140704 (10) AB 123

❤ *Filthy Coupon Request* ❤

Foreplay: Sexy biting for as long as we can.

Present this coupon to your other half (during an argument is probably not the best time). Vouchers can be used more than once in instances where both parties have thoroughly enjoyed the filthy activities that the said coupon has suggested. These coupons are for the sole pleasure of a consenting couple. They are fully flexible and can be interpreted by each couple as they please.

(01) 0 9501101 53000 3 (17) 140704 (10) AB 123

♡ Filthy Coupon Request ♡

You are going to cum all over my face tonight.

Present this coupon to your other half (during an argument is probably not the best time). Vouchers can be used more than once in instances where both parties have thoroughly enjoyed the filthy activities that the said coupon has suggested. These coupons are for the sole pleasure of a consenting couple. They are fully flexible and can be interpreted by each couple as they please.

(01) 0 9501101 53000 3 (17) 140704 (10) AB 123

♡ Filthy Coupon Request ♡

I want to oil up & rub my tits over your dick & balls.

(01) 0 9501101 53000 3 (17) 140704 (10) AB 123

❤ *Filthy Coupon Request* ❤

Let's watch some squirting videos, then make me squirt.

(01) 0 9501101 53000 3 (17) 140704 (10) AB 123

♡ Filthy Coupon Request ♡

Call me a slut/bitch while I sit on top of your dick. Pull my hair.

(01) 0 9501101 53000 3 (17) 140704 (10) AB 123

Filthy Coupon Request

Dominate me entirely. You are in charge tonight.

Present this coupon to your other half (during an argument is probably not the best time). Vouchers can be used more than once in instances where both parties have thoroughly enjoyed the filthy activities that the said coupon has suggested. These coupons are for the sole pleasure of a consenting couple. They are fully flexible and can be interpreted by each couple as they please.

(01) 0 9501101 53000 3 (17) 140704 (10) AB 123

Filthy Coupon Request

Role-play: Pretend you are my client. I am the prostitute. I am going to tell you about the two other guys I fucked before you.

(01) 0 9501101 53000 3 (17) 140704 (10) AB 123

Filthy Coupon Request

One buttocks massage for me.

(01) 0 9501101 53000 3 (17) 140704 (10) AB 123

❤ *Filthy Coupon Request* ❤

I want you to cum on my
feet/lips/tits/arse hole/ ....

(01) 0 9501101 53000 3 (17) 140704 (10) AB 123

Filthy Coupon Request

I want to suck you off while we watch porn. Get inspiration and direct me on whats next.

(01) 0 9501101 53000 3 (17) 140704 (10) AB 123

❤ Filthy Coupon Request ❤

Make me cum with your hands. Then I am
going to bring you close to cumming twice,
but you are not allowed to cum till I say.
Third time, I will sit on you or suck you
until you can't stop yourself anymore.

Present this coupon to your other half (during
an argument is probably not the best time).
Vouchers can be used more than once in
instances where both parties have thoroughly
enjoyed the filthy activities that the said
coupon has suggested. These coupons are for
the sole pleasure of a consenting couple. They
are fully flexible and can be interpreted by
each couple as they please.

(01) 0 9501101 53000 3 (17) 140704 (10) AB 123

♡ Filthy Coupon Request ♡

I am going to show you who my female crush is, then explain in detail what I want us to do together. Fuck me, while I whisper my dirty secrets. I know you would love to see me and another girl together.

(01) 0 9501101 53000 3 (17) 140704 (10) AB 123

♡ Filthy Coupon Request ♡

Roleplay: You, the pervy photographer, me as my sexy self. Take pictures of me.

Present this coupon to your other half (during an argument is probably not the best time). Vouchers can be used more than once in instances where both parties have thoroughly enjoyed the filthy activities that the said coupon has suggested. These coupons are for the sole pleasure of a consenting couple. They are fully flexible and can be interpreted by each couple as they please.

(01) 0 9501101 53000 3 (17) 140704 (10) AB 123

♡ Filthy Coupon Request ♡

Let's play Sex Charades. I will Wrap my hand around your penis. I wont say a word. I will give a little squeeze every time you do something that I really like until it turns into a full-on handjob for you.

(01) 0 9501101 53000 3 (17) 140704 (10) AB 123

♡ Filthy Coupon Request ♡

Slap my face and restrain me until I am so wet & you are so hard that we can't control ourselves anymore.

Present this coupon to your other half (during an argument is probably not the best time). Vouchers can be used more than once in instances where both parties have thoroughly enjoyed the filthy activities that the said coupon has suggested. These coupons are for the sole pleasure of a consenting couple. They are fully flexible and can be interpreted by each couple as they please.

(01) 0 9501101 53000 3 (17) 140704 (10) AB 123

♥ Filthy Coupon Request ♥

Two holes filled. Either with dicks. Or you and a toy/fingers while talking about getting another man to fuck me in front on you.

(01) 0 9501101 53000 3 (17) 140704 (10) AB 123

♡ Filthy Coupon Request ♡

I want you to kneel over me with your balls & dick in my face. I am going to touch myself until I cum, while I have your balls in my mouth. Then I will let you have your way with me.

Present this coupon to your other half (during an argument is probably not the best time). Vouchers can be used more than once in instances where both parties have thoroughly enjoyed the filthy activities that the said coupon has suggested. These coupons are for the sole pleasure of a consenting couple. They are fully flexible and can be interpreted by each couple as they please.

(01) 0 9501101 53000 3 (17) 140704 (10) AB 123

♡ Filthy Coupon Request ♡

Morning sex: Wake me up by caressing my body and slowly pushing your cock inside me. Don't say a word.

(01) 0 9501101 53000 3 (17) 140704 (10) AB 123

Filthy Coupon Request

ME/YOU BLINDFOLDED. NAKED.

Present this coupon to your other half (during an argument is probably not the best time). Vouchers can be used more than once in instances where both parties have thoroughly enjoyed the filthy activities that the said coupon has suggested. These coupons are for the sole pleasure of a consenting couple. They are fully flexible and can be interpreted by each couple as they please.

(01) 0 9501101 53000 3 (17) 140704 (10) AB 123

♡ *Filthy Coupon Request* ♡

SEX IN A ROOM WE DON'T USUALLY HAVE SEX IN.

(01) 0 9501101 53000 3 (17) 140704 (10) AB 123

♡ Filthy Coupon Request ♡

Golden shower. Me over you
or you over me. (we can do
it in the bath maybe?)

(01) 0 9501101 53000 3 (17) 140704 (10) AB 123

♡ Filthy Coupon Request ♡

Roleplay: Who's a naughty kitty?
I/you dress up as a sexy feline. Ears,
tails & everything

(01) 0 9501101 53000 3 (17) 140704 (10) AB 123

❤ *Filthy Coupon Request* ❤

Cover me/you in chocolate/icecream & lick it off.

(01) 0 9501101 53000 3 (17) 140704 (10) AB 123

❤ *Filthy Coupon Request* ❤

LET'S GO SHOPPING FOR A NEW SEX TOY TO USE TONIGHT.

Present this coupon to your other half (during an argument is probably not the best time). Vouchers can be used more than once in instances where both parties have thoroughly enjoyed the filthy activities that the said coupon has suggested. These coupons are for the sole pleasure of a consenting couple. They are fully flexible and can be interpreted by each couple as they please.

(01) 0 9501101 53000 3 (17) 140704 (10) AB 123

♡ Filthy Coupon Request ♡

I want us to

....

....

Present this coupon to your other half (during an argument is probably not the best time). Vouchers can be used more than once in instances where both parties have thoroughly enjoyed the filthy activities that the said coupon has suggested. These coupons are for the sole pleasure of a consenting couple. They are fully flexible and can be interpreted by each couple as they please.

(01) 0 9501101 53000 3 (17) 140704 (10) AB 123

♡ *Filthy Coupon Request* ♡

I want you to

....

....

Present this coupon to your other half (during an argument is probably not the best time). Vouchers can be used more than once in instances where both parties have thoroughly enjoyed the filthy activities that the said coupon has suggested. These coupons are for the sole pleasure of a consenting couple. They are fully flexible and can be interpreted by each couple as they please.

(01) 0 9501101 53000 3 (17) 140704 (10) AB 123

Filthy Coupon Request

I want to

....

....

Present this coupon to your other half (during an argument is probably not the best time). Vouchers can be used more than once in instances where both parties have thoroughly enjoyed the filthy activities that the said coupon has suggested. These coupons are for the sole pleasure of a consenting couple. They are fully flexible and can be interpreted by each couple as they please.

(01) 0 9501101 53000 3 (17) 140704 (10) AB 123

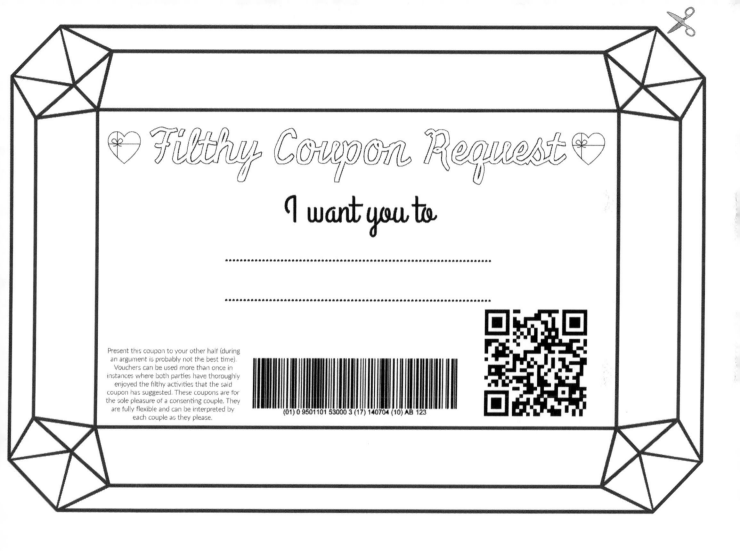

Filthy Coupon Request

I want you to

....

....

Present this coupon to your other half (during an argument is probably not the best time). Vouchers can be used more than once in instances where both parties have thoroughly enjoyed the filthy activities that the said coupon has suggested. These coupons are for the sole pleasure of a consenting couple. They are fully flexible and can be interpreted by each couple as they please.

(01) 0 9501101 53000 3 (17) 140704 (10) AB 123

Made in United States
Troutdale, OR
03/07/2024

18272904R00058